NATIVE AMERICAN HERBAL DISPENSATORY

The Guide to Producing Medication for Common Disorders and Radiant Health (2022 for Beginners)

Ted Waters

Table of Contents

NATIVE AMERICAN HERBAL DISPENSATORY

INTRODUCTION

A growing number of health-conscious clients are taking botanical supplements as more individuals become convinced of the medicinal potential of various roots and leaves.

"Yet, scientific investigation is still confined to only a handful of the hundreds of substances advertised in health food stores," stated the study's lead author, Andrea Borchers, PhD, a nutritional researcher at the University of California, Davis, and colleagues.

Native Americans used seven of the top 10 best-selling botanicals in the United States as medicines. Many of these supplements' stated benefits are based on what these early Americans utilized them for. However, nothing is known about how they used these medications, including plant-collection activities, exact plant components employed, and preparation methods.

The ancient North American inhabitants' usage of therapeutic herbs was "by no means haphazard, but quite discriminating." They made extensive use of some plant families while ignoring others. In truth, they employed diverse plant components to treat various ailments, combined many botanicals for specific therapeutic goals, and classified dangerous plants as poisons and medicines.

"The fact that Native Americans used so many botanicals in such a sophisticated manner suggests that among the products they used, there are some highly promising chemicals." However, very little scientific research has been conducted on any of these compounds thus far.

Both Echinacea (purple coneflower) and Urtica dioica (stinging nettle) have been examined, and there is evidence that both have medicinal characteristics.

"There is pretty strong evidence that all Echinacea species help to reduce symptoms of common colds, flu, and upper respiratory infections."

This, however, is not a consistent finding. What makes matters more complicated is that the extracts utilized in the studies came from different species or locations of the plants. They get a different chemical structure when they use the roots than when they use the plant's higher regions."

Scientists are still puzzled as to how Echinacea works in the body: "It appears to affect the immune system... and so helps the body fight off a cold or flu."

Echinacea is a herb that can be used instead of anti-flu medications. "It has been proved to be relatively safe due to considerable research with few adverse effects." " And it might even help."

Preliminary research on stinging nettle, which is commonly used to treat arthritis, suggests it has anti-inflammatory properties. "Because the research has only been done on animals, the image is much less clear." "There's always the question of how far animal studies can be extrapolated to human studies."

Certain research, however, "tend to validate what Native Americans observed" - that stinging nettle works.

Several studies have found that it directly inhibits some of the enzymes involved in inflammatory reactions.

In recent years, American manufacturers have failed to create consistent dosing for these botanicals. Because so little is known about Echinacea's active components, companies are having difficulties establishing a standard dose. "They don't even know what the ultimate active components are." Furthermore, there are still questions concerning how well these compounds are absorbed.

"European firms have been in this area much longer, and they have been pushing for standards for 15 or 20 years." This is a somewhat subjective perspective, but if you choose a European brand, you should get what they say is in there.

If you're determined to buy American-made goods, a well-known brand is your best choice. "There's talk about extract standardization and enhanced FDA control," but until that happens, you should search for anything else to base your purchasing decision on. If you're currently on medication and want to try a herbal, "there's the question of drug interaction, such as with St. John's Wort, which had negative reactions with transplant and HIV medicines." "While testing for drug interactions is still in its early stages, individuals who take many drugs should be aware of the different side effects of what they're taking."

While researchers have learned a lot about how Echinacea works in the body, he adds that there is still a lot to learn about the optimal dosage and the best type of preparation, whether it's a tincture, tea, capsule, or extract.

"Echinacea is worth taking, especially if you feel like you're becoming sick," he says. But, he cautions, don't mistake it for cold treatment.

"People make the mistake of treating Echinacea like vitamin C, taking it all the time during the cold and flu season," he says. "It stimulates the immune system, which is how it works." It is only effective for a short period and requires repeated administration.

"After two or three weeks of taking Echinacea every morning for two months, your immune system would stop responding to the stimulation." Three clinical studies have been published to back up this assertion. Take it for a maximum of two or three weeks."

CHAPTER 1: NATIVE AMERICAN MEDICINE

Native American medicine comprises the health practices of over 500 tribes. The specific strategies used by tribes differed, but they were all based on the basic principle that man is a part of nature and that health is a question of balance. The natural world drives when its interrelationships are recognized, promoted, and maintained in balance. The natural world is not visible to the naked eye and is unaffected by technology, but it may be felt directly and instinctively. Nature, like the inner life of a human person, has enormous forces that must be balanced in order to maintain equilibrium. Native medicine has been practised for 40,000 years. Because documentation has only recently begun, it is limited to observations, which is insufficient. Native medicine honours all of creation and is more than a body of knowledge or practice. Native American elders rarely share their knowledge out of fear of being exploited. Native American medicine focuses on finding balance in one's inner and outside lives. Body, mind, spirit, emotions, social group, and manner of life are all taken into account. In order to achieve harmony, a patient's preferences and decisions must always be honoured.

Each Native American healer has their own method, which may include bodywork, bone setting, midwifery, naturopathy, hydrotherapy, botanical and nutritional medicine, and so on. Ceremonial and ritual medicine are also available. Much of this has been lost because the only way this unrecorded living tradition has been perpetuated is via the efforts of living practitioners. Native Americans are becoming more concerned with preserving their culture, and as a result, Native American medicine is as adaptable today as it has always been.

Native American medicine is based on widely held beliefs about healthy living, the effects of disease-causing behaviour, and spiritual principles that restore balance. These ideas are shared by all tribes; nevertheless, diagnosis and treatment approaches vary greatly from tribe to tribe and healer to healer.

Native American healing traditions have been used in North America for at least 12,000 years, and maybe for 40,000 years. Although Native

American medicine indicates a standardized healing system, North America is home to around 500 indigenous peoples, each with its own set of healing knowledge, rituals, and ceremonies.

Many components of Native American healing have remained hidden and undocumented. The traditions are transmitted orally through elders, vision quests, and initiation. It is thought that disseminating therapeutic knowledge too publicly or casually can impair the spiritual efficacy of the medicine.

Many Native American healers, on the other hand, understand that writing down their healing processes is one way to ensure that these traditions are passed down to future generations. Many people believe that through sharing their healing methods and concepts, everyone will be able to reach a healthy balance with nature and all forms of life.

Native American medicine can help everyone who wishes to live a complete and balanced life. These benefits could be physical, emotional, or spiritual in nature. There is a general understanding, however, that "civilizational ailments," or white man's sicknesses, frequently necessitate white man's medication. In some cases, Native American medicine can be a vital component of a holistic approach to healing. For example, the most successful alcoholism treatment programs in Native communities have combined Western procedures with psychiatric counselling, social work, and traditional Native American healing traditions.

Native American medicine has a tough time treating inherited issues such as birth defects or retardation. Some diseases, according to native healers, are caused by a patient's behaviour. They will occasionally refuse to treat a patient if it interferes with their need to learn life lessons. Other illnesses are not treated because they are seen as "callings" or "initiation sicknesses." "The calling manifests itself in the form of a dream, accident, sickness, injury, disease, near-death experience, or even actual death," reveals Native healer Medicine Grizzly Bear Lake.

Native American medicine is based on a spiritual perspective of reality. A healthy person is someone who has a sense of purpose and follows the instructions of the Great Spirit. This advice is written in everyone's heart. To be healthy, one must commit to a path of beauty, harmony, and balance. A healthy life is also regarded to necessitate gratitude, respect, and charity. According to Ken Cohen, "health" entails "restoring the body, mind, and spirit to balance and wholeness: the balance of life energy in the body; the balance of ethical, reasonable, and just conduct; balanced links within family and community; and harmonious ties with nature."

Sickness causes, as well as disease nomenclature, varied from tribe to tribe.

Diseases are thought to have internal, external, or both causes.

Negative thinking, according to Cherokee medicine man Rolling Thunder, is the most important internal cause of disease. Shame, guilt, low self-esteem, avarice, despair, concern, melancholy, fury, envy, and self-centeredness are all examples of negative thinking. "No terrible sorcerer can cause you as much pain as you may cause yourself," Johnny Moses, a Nootka healer, says.

Diseases, like everything else, have extrinsic causes. "Germs are also spirits," says Shabari Bird of the Lakota Nation.

If a person's life is unbalanced, they have a weak constitution, they engage in negative thinking, or they are under stress, they are more prone to dangerous viruses. An illness could also be caused by other people or spirits. Poisons in the environment are another source of illness. Toxins include alcohol, polluted air, water, and certain foods.

Physical, emotional, or spiritual stress, according to Native American healers, can also trigger the sickness.

These traumatic experiences can result in mental and emotional distress, soul loss, and spiritual power loss. In these instances, the healer must use rituals and other ways to physically return the patient's soul and power. Some diseases are caused by those who break

the "laws of life." These guidelines may include considerations for animals, people, places, ritual artifacts, events, or spirits.
To diagnose ailments, Native American healers employ a range of techniques.
Examples include a discussion of one's symptoms, personal and family history, analysis of nonverbal cues such as posture or tone of voice, and medical divination.
The intuition, sensitivity, and spiritual strength of the healer are more important than the precise technique.

A typical Native American healing session does not exist. Prayer, chanting, music, smudging (burning sage or aromatic woods), herbs, laying-on of hands, massage, counselling, imagery, fasting, harmonizing with nature, dreaming, sweat lodges, taking hallucinogens (e.g., peyote), developing inner silence, embarking on a shamanic journey, and ceremony are all forms of healing.

Many healing sessions include members of the family and the community. Healing can happen quickly at times. It is not uncommon for healing to take a long period. The intensity of the therapy is regarded to be more important than the length of time required. Even though the recovery is swift, a lifestyle adjustment is frequently required to ensure that the healing is permanent.

A medicine bundle can also be used in Native American healing. The medicine bundle is a pouch made of leather or animal fur in which the healer keeps ritual objects, charms, herbs, stones, and other healing accoutrements. The bundle is a physical depiction of the medical power conferred by the spirits to the healer, either for general healing or for curing a specific illness. Bundles vary according to clan, tribe, and individual.

Native American medicine is not covered by insurance unless the practitioner is a qualified health care provider. The vast majority of Native healers do not charge a set fee for their services. Healing is thought to be a "gift from the Great Spirit." Gifts to the healer, on the other hand, are highly valued. Giving a gift "guarantees the efficacy of treatment since healing spirits adore generosity." Gifts can be groceries, clothing, money, or another personal expression of respect and appreciation. Often, a pouch of tobacco is all that is required as a gift.

Treatment Approach

Native American medicine is a comprehensive system that balances all aspects of a person's existence, from their inner world to their lifestyle and social ties.

Native medicine believes that the spiritual world is the source of all imbalances. Spiritual therapies are essential components of any treatment regimen.

Treatment approaches, including fees and pricing, are always precisely and uniquely created for the patient.

As part of the healing process, they incorporate the process of negotiating a cost. The healing Elder possesses the most healing power, and when therapy fails, the elder practitioner's reputation as a powerful healer suffers. The healing client makes an offer to the medical practitioner and waits to see if it is accepted. They never bargain face to face. The customer leaves the offering outside the healer's door, and if it is still there in the morning, it indicates that the offering was not accepted, and the client may proceed elsewhere.

Once they agree, treatment may begin with a behavioral prescription, such as commitment, selfless deeds, making amends, or hiking a sacred mountain.

Self-inquiry and discovery techniques are used to determine whether a lifestyle change, herbs, prayer, massage, a sweat lodge ritual, or a vision quest are required.

Theories

The holistic method focuses on improving the patient's view of the world around him by promoting a healthier self-concept, greater appreciation for others, and behavioral changes.

The healer's purpose is not just to cure the disease but also to transform the patient through disease experience. Native American medicine incorporates both technology and spirit with the advent of contemporary technologies.

Herbal therapies, as well as medications, are used. To give an example of a native medicine story, consider Barb, a wife, mother, and lawyer still battling breast cancer.

Despite doing everything she could, both naturally and artificially, cancer spread. He wanted to know what she had been doing or what hadn't changed in her life when they met in a sweat lodge with an Indian elder named Big Nose. She thought she was a failure as a mother, wife, lawyer, and now as a healer. Big Nose warned her that she needed to quit her negative self-talk. Barb chose to let go of her arrogant belief that she would be healed and instead appreciate the present moment with her family due to this meeting. Another anecdote tells of a woman who had severe arthritis and was always looking for the proper healer. Medicine men go deeper and beyond the situation at hand, realizing that significant change is sometimes required to assist healing. Herbs, massage, and prayer are secondary to the improvements. Right relationships and rectifying relationships with oneself, family, community members, and the spiritual world are all repercussions of relationship disruption and cause sickness.

Meanings of the Four Directions

The commitment to live in harmony with nature, self, community, and spirit is at the heart of the Shamanic path.

The four directions depict the Medicine Wheel or Wheel of Life: it symbolizes the life cycle, with no beginning or end, and provides advice for living. While the Medicine Wheel differs from culture to culture, it acknowledges the basic notion that all things on Earth are alive and interrelated. The simplest way to envision all Four Directions is on a wheel, with Spirit at the center. This wheel is known as "The Medicine Wheel" by Native Americans. Each direction is associated with a season, color, qualities, plants, and animals.

The four directions, as taught by Native American knowledge, are rich in symbolism and transformational guidance:

East

The East denotes Spring and is associated with victory, success, and power. After a long winter, there is a renewed sense of life. The color is red, and it represents protection. Red beads were used to summon the red spirit to have strong love relationships, heal from illness, and pray for long life. Birds in flight, such as the owl, hawk, and hummingbird, are East animals. Words are given to the East for them to fly and soar with Spirit.

The rising sun's orientation, East, indicates a new beginning, a new vision, rebirth, and ascension. The East Element is air, which governs our thinking, insight, and learning processes. Bird pictures, incense, and feathers

can all be used to represent the East. The season is spring when the earth awakens from its slumber and begins to restore the land's beauty. It's getting heated again. We're feeling energized and inventive.
Eastern energies project psychic abilities and excite the imagination.

Scent-based rituals and spells create a stronger connection to this Cardinal Direction. Aromas can be used in rituals to promote independence, open-mindedness, and self-development. Consider the East's freshness and a lightness of spirit.

East is the province of fairies and sylphs, lovely if whimsical creatures. They can be seen in the East at dawn and dusk (the inbetween times). Pale yellow (like the rising sun) and white are colors associated with the East. Gemini, Libra, and Aquarius are Zodiac signs that fall within this domain.

North

North denotes winter, as well as difficulties, challenges, and grief. Winter is a season of waiting and survival. Therefore the Cherokee term for North means "cold." North is represented by the color blue. White buffalo, moose, and bear are among the creatures that signify the North. These creatures serve as a reminder to be patient with the changing of the seasons.

The Cardinal Direction of North, like the North Star, is a guiding light. The energy of discoveries, grasp of deeper mysteries, deductive reasoning and logic, and pure intelligence can all be found here.

North is represented by Earth, which grounds us, provides for us, and vibrates on a prosperous level. Herbs, wood, stone, and flowers may be used in magical workings in the northern quadrant. The direction of North is likewise aligned with salt, which purifies.

The mystical beings who live in the North are people who have a strong connection to the land. Gnomes, Dwarves, and Trolls like the beautiful ambiance of a deep tunnel filled with natural scents. North denotes the hour of midnight and the winter season. In the cycle of days, midnight is a very potent time. The veils between realms thin during his hour, and we can see and experience things that would otherwise be hidden.

North is represented by the hues black, green, and brown. Taurus, Virgo, and Capricorn are Zodiac signs that are influenced by the North. Prosperity, grounding, spiritually-oriented herbalism, and binding are all magical works that benefit from the Northern quarter.

West

At the end of a cycle, West depicts Autumn and the final harvest. The West is black, and it symbolizes the end of the summer cycle. The west animals include the beaver, which represents teamwork in preparation for winter, and the snake, which represents how to lose our old skin in preparation for metamorphosis. West is the direction of enlightenment in China. Moving westward, according to Judaism, draws us closer to the illuminating presence of the

Divine. Both the Aztec civilization and the ancient Egyptians believed that here was the location of the portal to the next world. The Celtic tradition is similar, except that you must journey to the edge of the sea to find the nether world. People in India worship facing West, the direction of Mecca.

West, from a magical standpoint, represents the element of Water.

This is the unadulterated force of our emotional lives. Seasonally, West is the Fall, when the earth prepares for the winter's sleep and metamorphosis. People in the West use magic to break free from old habits, hurts, or patterns holding them back. According to Light Workers, the West is the most important direction to start a vision quest.

You may depict the west with numerous symbols such as a fish tank, a blue tablecloth, a cup, and seashells. The West direction in Ritual fosters our intuitive self, our ability to love, and our fertility.

This impact is felt in the astrological signs of Pisces, Scorpio, and Cancer.

South

The South represents summer, and it is a time of abundant abundance. Summer is a time of fertility, passion, development, joy, and tranquility. White is the color. The creatures of the South teach us about strength, courage, and pride. The eagle, with her great vision, and the wolf, who is glad to be a member of the tribe.

Moving to the southern region of creation, we have fire energy and high sun in the sky. This sheds light on concerns of the heart, in particular. The pulse of creation is waiting for a spark of life to form here. Summer is dominated by the South, and its colors are yellow and green. Sagittarius, Leo, and Aries are the zodiac signs connected with the South.

South represents our inner kid, who is alive and curious, in the human cycle. This child wants to be able to experience everything through their senses. Life is active here, and it is both energetic and joyful. Whereas other directions are more mental in nature, the South fosters spontaneity; it is physical and self-assured.

This quarter's colors include orange, gold, and yellow tones. The Djinn, Salamanders, the Great Red Dragon, and the Eternal Phoenix are the fantasy creatures that call this place home. Lizards, tigers, and the golden lion are natural animals associated with the South. Cleansing, protection, victory, and banishing negativity are all appropriate sorts of magic for the southern quadrant of your holy place. The South may also inspire faith, courage, and passion. Take a chance and take a leap of faith!

The Fundamentals of Native American Cardinal Directions

Direct transmission from Native wisdom provided the following symbolic features for the meaning of cardinal directions:

Honoring the East: Awakening, Ascension, Vision, and Spiritual Wisdom. At the crack of the morning, this is where the new beginnings of creation stir. With the rising sun comes the awakening of a greater spiritual consciousness. As the new warmth presses against us, our own divine spark ignites, and we become conscious of far more potential in life than we were previously. The intangible self lives vibrantly and scintillates with creative understanding in this spiritually centered region.

Honoring the West: Conclusions, stability, goals, foundations, and physical wisdom are important considerations.

When we follow the path of the setting sun, our gaze is drawn to the earth's surface. With this earthy, grounded vision, we consider the material and the wealth borne from matter's mouth. The roots of our bodies combine with mass — with the earth – in this physically oriented sector. We comprehend the concepts of totality and completion. We are also aware of the cycles of physical return.

Honoring the North: Illumination, discovery, logic, comprehension, and mental wisdom

Science and information acquired during our lifetimes is refined and trickles from the peaks of wisdom's ice-capped mountains. We prepare for Intellectual enlightenment when these streams of knowledge enter our awareness. The greatest reaches of our cognition roll back into us in this cognitively focused area, generating avalanches of deductive reasoning. Intellectual understanding is being digested and crystallized.

Honoring the South: Empathy, Trust, Faith, Inclusion, Love, Emotional wisdom
A journey through ethereal bloodlines unveils the symphony of shifting emotions. We immerse ourselves in revitalizing waters, leaning into the cosmic aortic pulse.

Each beat of our collective heart stirs our life waters, and we experience wholeness as a result. We softly feel our way into a larger current in this emotionally driven region. We comprehend the concept of unity. We swim smoothly among the community, following the rivers of love and the least amount of opposition.

Healing Plants

When we feature medicinal plants native to our North American homes, we combine Mother Earth Living's dual focuses on natural health and local eating. In keeping with nature's remarkable ability to provide for our well-being, each region of the world has its own healing plants. Much of our traditional plant knowledge in North America comes from the American Indians, who relied on medicinal plants for much of their health care. However, comprehending American Indian medicinal herb utilization is difficult.

First, the use of medicinal plants varies greatly across the numerous tribes—and knowledge of these plants' functions is typically culturally guarded. While many of us are aware of botanical immune boosters like echinacea and elderberry, or the skin-soothing effect of witch hazel (to mention a few), there are countless other North American plants with strong medical roots. People have required plants since the beginning of time, not only for existence but also to enrich their lives and make the act of living a little more comfortable.

Here are some plants whose traditional uses by the indigenous peoples of this continent continue to inform and affect how we treat diseases and maintain human health.

General precaution: Before using herbal products, we always recommend that you contact a trained healthcare practitioner, especially if you are pregnant, nursing, or taking any drugs.

California Poppy

Even the roots, blooms, and seedpods, which have a vivid orange color, may be utilized for therapeutic purposes.

To get rid of head lice, the Costanoan tribe used a powerful tea made from the blossoms. They used the seeds to make a hair tonic dressing for the Ohlone people.

Various tribes in the Mendocino area drank the roots to treat a wide range of ailments, from headaches to stomachaches to dental pains, while nursing mothers would wash their breasts with root juice to help dry the flow of milk when it was time to wean their babies.

Pomo women made strong teas from the seedpods and applied them to their breasts for the same purpose.

Gooseberry & Currants

Currants and gooseberries have long been utilized medicinally by indigenous peoples in North America. To ease irritated throats, the Comanche utilized berry tea as a gargle. The Prairie Potawatomi people used the root to make a decoction used as an eyewash to eliminate foreign particles or relieve tired or sore eyes. The Muscogee (Creek) people drank a powerful tea produced from the root bark to eliminate intestinal worms. Gooseberry juice was also used as a wash on the skin to heal irritated and inflamed skin tissue.

Milkweed

Several Native cultures have employed the milkweed latex fluid from the roots, plant tops, and stems for medicinal purposes. The latex was used by the Miwok people to remove warts. To treat snow blindness, the Cheyenne created a decoction of the dried plant tops and used it as an eyewash. Pleurisy root, also known as butterfly milkweed (Asclepias tuberosa), was utilized as a cough cure by the Cherokee, Delaware, and Mohegan peoples.

Nettles

The Hesquiaht and Miwok peoples employed nettles to treat muscular and joint discomfort, sometimes by whipping fresh nettle stems over the injured body parts. When the formic acid came into contact with the skin, it caused brief burning and blistering, but it also caused a surge of circulation to those areas. This increased circulation in the muscles and joints provided some long-term pain alleviation for illnesses such as arthritis. The Cherokee made nettle tea and drank it as a stomach tonic. During birthing, the Cree Indians believed nettles to be a vital women's herb.

Echinacea

Plant Family: Asteraceae
Botanical Name
Echinacea purpurea (L.) Moench
Standardized: Echinacea purpurea

Other: Purple coneflower

Echinacea is one of the most well-known herbal treatments in folk herbalism in the United States. Echinacea has been widely used by herbalists and American Indians in North America for decades, and it acquired favor in Europe in the 1900s. Although many of its past uses were related to topical treatments, one of its principal functions is to enhance good immunological function.

It is now one of the most widely available dietary supplements in health food stores and ongoing scientific research.

There are nine native species in the United States and Canada, with a high prevalence in Kansas, Arkansas, Oklahoma, and Missouri. These perennial members of the sunflower (Asteraceae) family enjoy rocky, disturbed soils in open fields, grasslands, and beside railroad tracks. E. purpurea, E. angustifolia, and E. pallida are the most common species found in trade.

Echinacea is derived from the Greek word echinos, which means hedgehog, and alludes to the spiny seed head. Although E. purpurea is the most frequently cultivated species, it is increasingly rare in the wild due to overharvesting. Growing E. pallida and E. Angustifolia is more difficult.

Uses and Preparations
• Fresh or dried root can be used to make tea, tincture, or capsules.
• Fresh or dried aboveground parts as tea, tincture, or capsules.
• Juice from fresh plants.

Precautions

People who are allergic to other members of the Asteraceae family should be cautious.

Folklore and History of Echinacea

American Indians and traditional herbalists in North America used echinacea extensively. Several tribes, notably the Pawnee, Dakota, and Omaha-Winnebago, relied significantly on this herb, which was utilized for maladies ranging from immune system support to horse distemper.

In the late 1800s, American Eclectic physicians championed echinacea, with a focus on Echinacea Angustifolia. Eclectics such as John Uri Lloyd and John King exalted its advantages to such an extent that it became the Eclectics' single most widely used herb. It was popular until the Eclectic schools disbanded in the mid-1930s.

Black Cohosh
Standardized: Black cohosh
Other: rattlesnake root, rattleweed, squawroot, Black bugbane, black snakeroot, rheumatism weed, bugwort, rattle root, rattle snakeroot,
Plant Family: Ranunculaceae
Botanical Name: Actaea racemosa (L.)

The flowering perennial black cohosh is endemic to much of Canada and the United States. It flourishes in old-growth coastal forests and areas with high biodiversity. The United States and Canada produce and cultivate the great majority of the world's black cohosh. The plant can reach 3 to 6 feet and has a stalk covered in tiny white flowers. Between late July and September is the optimal time to harvest the therapeutic root.

It was a popular herbal cure among American Indians, who utilized it to treat many diseases. The word is derived from the Algonquian tribe and means "rough," referring to the rhizome's texture. Because the blossoms have such a strong stench, it was given the moniker "bugbane," and it has been used to repel insects effectively.

Black cohosh has long been used to promote women's health, and it has been approved by Germany's Commission E for premenstrual discomfort and pain linked with natural menstruation. Black cohosh can also help with healthy menopause.

Uses and Preparations

Dried root in tablets, Finely chopped, teas or tinctures

Precautions

Do not confuse with blue cohosh, which can be harmful. Pregnancy should only be used under

the supervision of a skilled healthcare
practitioner.

Black Cohosh Effectiveness

In his famous reference book Herbal Medicine, Dr. Rudolph Weiss cites black cohosh as a treatment for disorders induced by a lack of estrogen, such as menopausal depression.

This is supported by the clinical experience of European practitioners. According to scientific evidence, black cohosh has a balanced influence on hormone production, either by functioning as a weak estrogen or by regulating estrogen production in the body. As a result, black cohosh is frequently used in herbal formulae for female hormone regulation, particularly those suggested to prevent hot flashes, which can occur when estrogen levels fall too low.

Commercial formulations of the herb, which are accessible in the US, are routinely prescribed in Europe and are supported by several test-tube and animal studies and a few human trials.

In one controlled, double-blind research, a standardized black cohosh extract was given to 110 menopausal women who complained of unpleasant symptoms and had not used estrogen replacement therapy for at least six months. According to the researchers, the women felt less unhappy and had fewer hot flashes than those in the placebo group.

Cranberry
Plant Family: Ericaceae
Standardized: Cranberry
Botanical Name
Vaccinium macrocarpon
Other: American cranberry, large cranberry

The traditional Thanksgiving side dish is also one of the most versatile antimicrobial herbs. Cranberry has anti-asthmatic and diuretic properties in addition to its traditional usage in treating urinary tract infections. Cranberry is a North American native fruit, with over 98 percent of the world's supply grown in the northern United States and Canada.

Cranberry was appreciated by both indigenous Americans and colonists for its medicinal and nutritional virtues. Cranberries are a high-value crop, ranking 40th in cash crop sales tracked by the USDA's National Agricultural Statistical Service.

Uses and Preparations

The powdered berry is best for therapeutic purposes. It can be ingested or mixed into sugar-free teas. Most dried and powdered items on the market are freeze-dried and typically contain an anticaking chemical to avoid solidification.

Precautions

There are no precautions.

Cranberry Can Do!

These are the main medical properties of cranberry, according to the University of Maryland Medical Center.

1. **Prevent urinary tract infections:** Several studies have found that cranberries can help reduce bladder and urethral infections. When compared to a placebo, Cranberry juice reduced the number of bacteria in the bladder in one trial of elderly women. Another study found that younger women with a history of frequent UTIs who took cranberry capsules experienced fewer UTIs than those who received a placebo. However, research indicates that cranberry does not function once you have a UTI.

2. **Prevent ulcers:** According to two studies, Cranberry may help inhibit the bacteria Helicobacter pylori from sticking to stomach walls. Because H. pylori can cause stomach ulcers, cranberries may help prevent stomach ulcers.

3. **Ward off cancer:** Some in vitro and animal research suggest that cranberry may aid in the prevention of cancer cell growth.

4. **Fight viruses:** Cranberry appears to be effective against several viruses in test tubes. Human studies are required.

5. **Fight bacterial illness:** Cranberry has been found to suppress common bacterial strains such as E. coli and Listeria monocytogenes.

American Ginseng

Plant Family: Araliaceae
Other: Xi yang shen
Botanical Name: Panax quinquefolius (L.)
Standardized: American ginseng

Ginseng refers to three distinct herbs: Asian or Korean ginseng (Panax ginseng), American ginseng (P. quinquefolius), and Siberian "ginseng" (Eleutherococcus senticosus), the latter of which has many of the same benefits but belongs to a different plant family.
American ginseng is farmed along North America's whole eastern shore, from Quebec to Florida. As opposed to Asian ginseng, American ginseng has "cooling" characteristics and is known for its thirst-quenching benefits.

American Indians used it in the same way as Chinese people did, as a preventative measure. When it was discovered that ginseng grew wild in North America, it quickly became a lucrative business. Daniel Boone, an American folk hero and frontiersman, was a fur trader who made a fortune selling wild-harvested ginseng.

The great bulk of ginseng research has concentrated on the Asian type rather than the American. Herbalists frequently use the two species interchangeably since they have comparable characteristics. Ginseng has been recognized by the German Commission E for invigoration and fortification during times of necessity. It has been demonstrated that it improves response time and concentration in healthy adults. Ginseng has been demonstrated to improve healthy aging and memory in older persons.

Uses and Preparations
The dried mature root is utilized in teas, extracts, and capsules.

Precautions

Combination with warfarin should only be done under the direction of a skilled healthcare practitioner.

American Ginseng Benefits

Ginseng is occasionally referred to be an "adaptogen," which means it is a herb that helps the body deal with various types of stress, though there is no scientific evidence to support this claim. American ginseng has been shown in animal experiments to be useful in enhancing the immune system and as an antioxidant. Other research suggests that American ginseng may have antiinflammatory properties.

The following conditions have been studied:
Diabetes:

Several human investigations have shown that American ginseng decreases blood sugar levels in type 2 diabetics. The effect was noticed on both fasting and postprandial (after eating) glucose levels. According to one study, persons with type 2 diabetes who took American ginseng before or after a high-sugar drink had a lower increase in blood glucose levels. Other research suggests that North

American ginseng reduces stress and protects diabetes-related problems such as retinal and heart functioning abnormalities.

More investigation is required.

Cancer: Tumor growth has been demonstrated to be inhibited by American ginseng. American ginseng was discovered to have powerful anti-cancer effects in one laboratory study on colorectal cancer cells.

Colds and flu: In two studies, people who took the American ginseng supplement Cold FX for four months had fewer colds than those who took a placebo. Those who caught a cold had shorter symptoms than those who took a placebo.

ADHD: According to one exploratory study, American ginseng combined with Ginkgo biloba may help cure ADHD.

Immune system: Some researchers believe that American ginseng boosts the immune system, which could assist the body in fighting infection and sickness. Several clinical trials have demonstrated that American ginseng improves the performance of immune cells.

Persimmon

The Cherokee people harvested the fruits shortly before the first frost and used them to make an astringent medicinal syrup to treat diarrhea. For the same purpose, the Choctaw sun-dried the fruit and cooked it into bread.

The Catawba tribe used the fruit as a poultice to treat warts and a decoction of the tree's bark as a mouthwash for thrush (a type of fungal infection). The Rappahannock Indians consumed the bark to ease heartburn.

Spruce

Native Americans recognized that drinking tea made from spruce needles kept them well during the long, cold winters. Scurvy became a problem for colonists in Quebec City in the 1500s (caused by a vitamin C deficiency). This vital medicine was provided to them by the Iroquois Indians. Drinking spruce tea and spruce beer, known as Newfoundland spruce beer, cured them of scurvy and served as a crucial prophylactic measure.

Willow

Many tribes, including the Choctaw and Delaware Indians, employed peachleaf willow (S. amygdaloides) and other species to create a toothbrush out of a short willow twig. It would clean their teeth, and the tannins' astringency would help keep their gums healthy.

Yew

Women of the Okanagan tribe and other northwestern coastal tribes have traditionally used yew berries as contraception. The Quinault people decimated the bark and drank it in very small doses to treat arthritis, TB, and renal problems. The Cowlitz Indians used the needles to make a poultice and administered it topically to wounds. The leaves, on the other hand, are poisonous and should not be consumed.

Saw Palmetto

Botanical Name
Serenoa repens
Standardized: Saw palmetto
small plant Family: Arecaceae
Other: Sabal palm (W. Bartram)

Saw palmetto is a tiny palm species native to the southeastern United States, with a concentration in Florida and a few nearby areas.

Because they grow prostrate most of the time, the plants average three to six feet tall, rising to 15 feet on rare instances when they grow erect. Saw palmetto plants can live for hundreds of years; the oldest plants in Florida are thought to be between 500 and 700 years old. Saw palmetto grows in sandy soil and produces therapeutic fruit all summer and into October. When fully mature, the fruit is bluish-black. It has a unique, sweet scent, as well as a slightly soapy and bitter flavor.

Saw palmetto berries were employed as a food source and general tonic by American Indians in Florida, and early American settlers ate them to avoid famine. American botanist John Lloyd was among the first to notice the fruit's beneficial effects on grazing animals, believing that it may also benefit people. The herb fell out of favor in the 1950s because science couldn't explain the berries' observed actions.

Saw palmetto is now one of the most widely used and researched herbs for promoting good prostate function.

Uses and Preparations

Berries that have been dried and sliced or powdered are utilized in teas, tinctures, and encapsulations.

Precautions

No known precautions.

Does Saw Palmetto Really Work?

For more than a century, saw palmetto fruit extracts have been used to treat prostate disorders, particularly benign prostatic hyperplasia, or BPH. BPH is defined by a benign (noncancerous) enlargement of the prostate and is thought to affect more than half of men over 50. It causes decreased urine flow, which can result in various symptoms such as straining to urinate, uncomfortable urination, increased frequency of urination, and more.

More than two dozen controlled clinical investigations, most of which were conducted in Europe, support saw standardized palmetto extracts. Clinical trials have shown that palmetto is as effective as a conventional medication in relieving BPH symptoms while having fewer negative effects.

In June 1999, the findings of the first saw palmetto clinical trial in the United States was published. For six months, 44 men with BPH were given 320 mg per day of saw palmetto extract or a placebo. The size of prostate tissue was found to have shrunk from 17.8 percent to 10.7 percent in persons treated with saw palmetto, with virtually no known side effects. According to UCLA urologist Leonard Marks, the study's lead author, "saw palmetto extracts appear to be a reasonable therapy choice for males with simple symptomatic BPH."

Intersections o Traditional and Western Healing

Today, Native people of all ethnicities are frequently faced with using traditional Native healing methods or seeking Western medical therapy. Until recently, the two traditions existed in parallel, with little overlap. Native Americans, on the other hand, now have access to a full range of healthcare services. Many traditional healers continue to work on their own inside tribal groups. To coordinate care for Native American patients, other healers may collaborate with Westerntrained primary care physicians. Some healthcare facilities, frequently in the same area, provide both traditional and Western medicine.

Native American patients in most locations receive traditional healing from inside their local tribal community rather than via tribal health facilities or hospitals. Tribal people in the Dakota and Lakota and the Mandan, Hidatsa, and Arikara (MHA) Tribes of the Upper Plains arrange for services by contacting local healers directly. Some Western-trained physicians will also refer patients to traditional healers and will occasionally assist in coordinating both Western and traditional therapy for a specific patient.

The Waianae Coast Comprehensive Health Center

The Dr. Agnes Kalaniho'okaha Cope Native Hawaiian Traditional Healing Center, located in Waianae Coast Comprehensive Health on O'ahu, Hawai'i, offers a variety of traditional healing modalities led by master practitioners. The practices, located on-site alongside Western primary medical care and complete health and wellness services, are overseen by a Council of Elders.

Every practice begins with Pule and Oli (prayer and chant). The Traditional Healing Center's Native techniques include:

- Pule, healing through prayer
- Haha, healing through diagnostic observation

- He Ike Papalua, extrasensory perception or second sight
- Lomilomi, or Hawaiian massage
- La'au Lapa'au, healing with herbal medicine
- La'au Kahea, spiritual healing
- Pale Keiki, the art of midwifery
- Ho'oponopono, family conflict resolution and counseling

Southcentral Foundation

Southcentral Foundation in Anchorage, Alaska, has emerged as a pioneer in providing traditional healing treatments to supplement those provided by the largest Western medicine center, the Alaska Native Medical Center. In collaboration with Western-trained clinicians, the Traditional Healing Clinic provides traditional healing practices to patients upon request or referral. The clinic also provides Alaska Natives with a variety of wellness, lifestyle, and trauma rehabilitation services.

The Southcentral Foundation Traditional Healing Clinic received the Indian Health

Service Director's Special Recognition Award in June 2011 for demonstrating "how tribal doctors, elders, and traditional healing practices can work side by side with Western medicine...for the ultimate benefit of Native patients, families, and communities."

The Malcolm Baldridge National Quality Award was presented to the Southcentral Foundation in November 2011 to appreciate its extraordinary dedication to excellence and results in health care. The Nuka System of Care, which recognizes Alaska Native people as "customer-owners" and fosters strong relationships between consumers and health practitioners, personnel, and facilities, is key to SCF's success. "Medical, behavioral, dental, and traditional health practices, as well as supporting infrastructure, collaborate with the Native Community to promote physical, mental, emotional, and spiritual wellness."

One of Southcentral's programs, the Family Wellness Warriors Initiative, addresses domestic violence, abuse, and neglect in the

Alaska Native community. The program encourages male family members to restore their historical position as family protectors through ceremonial and group therapy sessions while also providing therapeutic themes of individual responsibility and redemption. The following Native traditions are available at the Southcentral Foundation Traditional Healing Clinic:

- Counseling
- Talking circles
- Medicinal garden
- Healing hands and healing touch
- Song and dance
- Prayer
- Cleansing

Caring for the "Invisible Tribe"

Two out of every three Native Americans now reside in cities rather than on tribal territories. Unfortunately, urban Indians sometimes do not have practical access to or lose eligibility for health care through tribal-managed systems or the US Indian Health Service. According to a 2007 assessment by the Urban Indian Health

Commission, their health is among the lowest of any ethnic community. While there is no national program to address the problems of the "Invisible Tribe," as urban Indians are frequently referred to, local efforts have produced some imaginative, therapeutic remedies to help medically disadvantaged Native Americans living in American cities.

The Seattle Indian Health Board and the Native American Health Center in Oakland, California, offer a full range of Western primary medical care and dental services to Native American patients.

They also promote community activities, revitalize Native pride, and enable patients to get traditional healing procedures. These two clinics are examples of creative initiatives to meet the medical and cultural requirements of the various Native Americans living in metropolitan cities.

A new Seven Directions Building with a Medicine Wheel design has been added to the Oakland facility. The name represents the Four + Three = Seven Directions (east, south, west, and north, plus above, on, and below the earth). The structure integrates housing, community development, and medical and dental facilities. Over 30 Urban Indian Health clinics are represented by the National Council of Urban Indian Health in the United States.

CHAPTER 2: HERBAL MEDICINE

For centuries, traditional herbal therapy has been used to meet the healthcare needs of civilizations all over the world.

Despite current medical and technological advancements, there is an increase in global demand for herbal medications. In actuality, it is estimated that this industry generates almost $60 billion per year.

Some natural remedies may be less expensive and easier to obtain than traditional pharmaceuticals, and many people prefer to use them because they align with their personal health goals. Nonetheless, you might be questioning if herbal options are beneficial.

Herbal medicine is the use of plants and plant extracts to treat disease. Many modern drugs were originally derived from plants, despite the fact that they are currently created synthetically. Herbal remedies utilise the complete plant, whereas Western medicine today focuses on the active ingredient. Herbalists believe that the combination of components in the entire plant (called synergy) performs better collectively than a single active element.

Is it secure?

Herbal medicines are generally safe, although they can have undesirable side effects. These symptoms can include stomach upset, sleeplessness, and muscle or joint pain. Some herbal medicines may interact with the pharmaceuticals you are taking.
If you're thinking about using these remedies, make sure you acquire them from a respected manufacturer to guarantee they're of high quality, and always consult with your doctor first.

A new method for regulating traditional herbal medicines went into effect in May 2014.
This is overseen by the MHRA, a government institution. It requires that herbal medicines sold in the UK have a long history of use, be of good quality, and be safe.

Sourcing Herbs

When acquiring bulk spices and herbs for your home herbal apothecary, it is critical to consider the growing procedures and storage practices of the companies you are purchasing. Like any other plant, herbs can be grown organically and with regenerative practices that improve and maintain soil quality, or they can be cultivated using pesticides.

Of course, it goes without saying that when it comes to procuring herbs for your own holistic health, it is critical that the herbs you purchase are cultivated organically and without the use of any dangerous chemicals that we do not want in our bodies or our herbal compositions. When looking for bulk spices and herbs, you may come across the word "wildcrafted," which refers to plants that have been gathered directly from their original, wild habitat. I'll go into how to wildcraft herbs later sustainably, but for now, I'd like to explain what this phrase implies because you're certain to come across it.

Wildcrafted herbs are gathered from a native forest, field or undeveloped location where the plants naturally grew. In other words, they were not grown commercially in a "farm" setting.

WILDCRAFTED HERBS VS. ORGANICALLY GROWN HERBS

There are many different opinions on whether wildcrafted herbs are a better option than organic. Still, in my opinion, it would be fantastic to use wildcrafted herbs and plants that you discover in your own natural habitat for your own personal house and use. As long as you can acquire wildcrafted herbs and plants in a way that does not harm the natural ecology (which we will discuss in a later post), I believe that wildcrafted herbs are a wonderful way to connect with your local environment and the plants that dwell there.

HERBAL ENERGETICS

Like all living organisms, herbs and plants are known in herbal medicine to contain their own intrinsic energy. This is especially relevant when comparing wildcrafted to organically grown herbs and plants because wildcrafted herbs live in harsher environments and are thus naturally conditioned to have more powerful energy.

Organically grown herbs and plants, on the other hand, are thought to be "coddled" and grown under ideal conditions that are in many ways controlled and improved by the farmer, leading many herbalists to argue that organically grown plants are simply not energetically capable of being all that they can be.

SUSTAINABLY SOURCING WILDCRAFTED HERBS

While most herbalists agree that in a perfect world, herbs and plants used for herbal medicine would be wildcrafted, the expansion of our globe's population and interest in herbal medicine (which is a wonderful thing!) makes it impossible for wildcrafted herbs to fulfill today's demands. Indeed, we have already begun to witness how commercial wildcrafting practices have placed a strain on wild plant species and put many at risk.

This is why, if you wish to wildcraft your herbs, you must verify that you are only picking species that are not vulnerable or endangered; organic commercial growing methods are the only alternative for these plants.

Guidelines for wildcrafting herbs

This may sound apparent, but one of the most important things to remember while wildcrafting herbs is to double-check your plant identification.

Knowing the Latin names of plants might be useful because common names can refer to more than one species. If you're unsure, botany or herbal book with clear descriptions, as well as images or drawings, might be quite helpful.

If you are harvesting an invasive weed, it may be an excellent opportunity to remove it while totally putting it to good use. Make sure to allow plenty of space for other plants so they can reproduce. Dry, sunny weather is ideal for wildcrafting. This is the time of year when volatile oil levels are at their maximum.

The countryside is an excellent spot to look for therapeutic herbs. Many farmers will let you gather rosehips, nettles, and other unpleasant herbs if you ask first. This allows you to check to see if they've been sprayed.

Many valuable plants grow in roadside ditches. However, they should be avoided because they will be covered with exhaust residue. They could have also been sprayed by the council. You might make an exemption if the road is exceptionally quiet and/or the plants are at least 10 meters away from passing traffic — and you know they haven't been sprayed.

Dry, sunny weather is ideal for foraging for herbs. This is the time of year when volatile oil levels are at their maximum. It also works nicely if you wish to dry your plants. It's quite convenient that the ideal weather for wildcrafting herbs is also good picnic weather.

Drying herbs

When selecting plants to harvest, look for those that are clean and have minimum damage. If you want to dry them, do so as soon as you can after picking them. All herbs must be dried in a shaded, wellventilated, and dry location. A shady part of a veranda is ideal. Berries like hawthorn and rosehip can be dehydrated or strung on dental floss or embroidery thread.

Roots should be washed or rinsed to remove dirt, but don't soak them because medicinal compounds can leach out into the water (this is particularly the case with milky roots like marshmallows). It will also make drying the roots more difficult. Large roots must be cut into smaller pieces around the one-inch length. After the outer covering has been removed, bulbs can be sliced.

Roots, bulbs, loose leaves, and flowers can be dried by spreading them out on paper, a screen, or a sheet or drying them in a dehydrator. Plants can also be hung in bunches upside down. When the stems become brittle and easily break, they are dry. Berries like hawthorn and rosehip can be dehydrated or strung on dental floss or embroidery thread.

Storage

Herbs should ideally be stored in dark brown jars with tight-fitting lids. If this isn't possible, use clear glass, but keep the jars in the dark cupboard. Label each jar with the herb's name and harvest date.

In a nutshell, wildcrafting herbs all year.
- Summer: blossoms (as they open), leaves, fruit (at peak ripeness)
- Autumn: (such as fennel), roots, seeds, hawthorn berries and rosehips
- Spring: young leaves (such as nettle)
- Winter: roots, chickweed

Wildcrafting herbs in autumn

The autumn season is best for digging most roots. At this time, many plants begin to concentrate their energy underground. Biennial roots, such as burdock, are best collected during their first year when the growth cycle is focused on the leaves and roots. In the second year, they blossom and go to seed.

A common dandelion root is an easy-to-find form of the root. True dandelions (Taraxacum officinal) have a hollow stem rising from a rosette of smooth leaves, but "false" dandelions (also known as catsear) have branched stems and slightly hairy leaves. Both are edible, so don't worry if you mix them up. Herbalists employ the "genuine" dandelion for medicinal purposes.

The autumn season is best for digging most roots.

Dandelions aid digestion, are high in minerals (especially vitamin A and iron) and are an excellent liver tonic.

They are also an excellent diuretic, can help clear up skin issues like dermatitis, and boost breast milk supply. In the summer, you can eat the leaves and blooms, and in the autumn and winter, you can eat the root. The root has a mildly bitter taste similar to that of a parsnip. Drinking dandelion coffee is one of the most popular methods to ingest dandelions. While this is readily available in stores, it might be enjoyable to make your own.

Dandelion coffee

Roasted dandelion tastes similar to coffee, but it stimulates the digestive system without stimulating the neurological system. To produce a jar of coffee, you'll need to dig up a lot of dandelion roots. Because the plant has extensive tap roots, be careful not to snap and lose part of them while digging. Once you have a nice pile of roots, scrub them and chop them into 1–2cm pieces.

The roots must then be dried. They will take a few hours to dehydrate in a dehydrator. Spread them out on clean paper or a sheet in a well-ventilated but shady location. Depending on the weather, they may take several days or even a few weeks to dry.

Preheat the oven to 200°C once the fabric has dried. Place the roots on a baking sheet and roast for 20–25 minutes. But keep an eye on them. Thinner parts will cook more quickly. They should be a dark brown color and completely dry.

Reduce the temperature of the oven to 180°C. Cool the roots before grinding them. A coffee or spice grinder is ideal for this, although a food processor would suffice.

Return the ground roots to the oven for 5 minutes.

Hips & berries

In the autumn, rosehips can be found all over the countryside. The majority of wild rosehips are from the Dog Rose (Rosa canina), the cultivar most widely utilized by herbalists. They are well recognized for their high vitamin C content. Still, they also include calcium and vitamins B, E, and K. Rosehip tea or syrup is commonly used to cure colds and coughs, not only because of the vitamin C content but also because it is somewhat astringent, which is beneficial for soothing sore throats.

Hips are ready to pick from late February to early May, with the finest months being March and early April. You can dry them and use them to make tea for months to come. The exterior meat and seeds are both nutritious, but the prickly hairs surrounding the seeds must be removed by grinding the whole, dried hips and passing them through a sieve. The hairs should all shake free of the hips — just don't grind the hips too fine or they'll pass through the sieve as well.

Hawthorn berries can also be gathered and dried in the autumn; however, avoid the toxic stones in the middle.

Hawthorn (Crataegus oxyacantha and Crataegus monogyna) is regarded as a heart tonic. It may take several months to notice an improvement, but it is widely known for its ability to normalize both high and low blood pressure. It can also help to normalize an irregular heartbeat. Bioflavonoids are abundant in hawthorn.

Wildcrafting herbs in winter
Winter is a slow season for wildcrafting herbs, although roots can still be harvested. Most leafy herbs must be harvested in the spring, with the notable exception of chickweed (Stellaria media). It flourishes in moderate climates during the winter.

It's generally too stringy to bother with by mid-spring. Like many medicinal plants, it is nutrientpacked, but unlike some medicinal plants (such as dandelion), it has a very mild and pleasant flavor. It is frequently enjoyed by children. Aside from tossing it into winter salads, chickweed can be used as a poultice for eye disorders, including conjunctivitis and pink eye. Because it shrinks so much when cooked, it is hardly worth cooking. You might add it at the end of a stir-fry or make wilted chickweed like this.

Wilted chickweed

Rinse and set aside several large handfuls of chickweed (leaves and stems). In a pan, melt a knob of butter over low heat. Add the chickweed and stir-fry just until it begins to wilt as it melts. A teaspoon of wholegrain mustard and a generous squeeze of lemon juice should be added. Give it one last swirl before turning off the heat. This goes well with bread or rice.

Wildcrafting herbs in spring

While it is still possible to collect roots in early spring, it is more season for fresh, green leaves. Good King Henry, nasturtium, borage, yellow dock, dandelion, chicory, fat hen, field mustard, and sorrel are some common (and frequently unwelcome) edible plants that may appear in your yard in the spring. All of these can be eaten in salads, though you may want to consume some of them sparingly because they have a variety of bitter, sour, and spicy flavors. Watercress can be found in streams. However, it must be cooked if there is any uncertainty about the quality of the water.

The tops of nettle plants (Urtica dioica) also make a fantastic spring herb, but they must be boiled or dried to remove the sting. They have a flavor similar to spinach and can be turned into a soup or tea.

In terms of nutrition, nettles are a bit of a superfood. They are also well-known as a blood purifier, kidney tonic, and beneficial supplement to take during pregnancy.

Try the following for an inexpensive, simple, and incredibly nutrient-dense meal.

Millet & wild herbs

- Prepare a serving of millet (or another grain such as rice or buckwheat).
- Gather a wide range of wild herbs in a large bowl in the yard or neighboring fields. Make cautious only to collect little amounts of the stronger-tasting herbs.
- Add a generous handful of milder-flavored herbs from the garden or refrigerator, such as parsley, coriander, and (if it's early spring) chickweed.
- A few green vegetable leaves, such as spinach or collards, can be added.
- Snip all of the greens into small pieces with a pair of scissors and toss everything together.
- Toss the greens and grains with tamari, pickled garlic, herbal or basic apple-cider vinegar, sesame oil, roasted sesame or sunflower seeds, and sesame oil.

Wildcrafting herbs in summer

Flowers such as clover, dandelion, calendula, borage, red and violet are best harvested in the summer. All of these blooms can be used to season salads. They are all useful in other ways as well. Borage blooms are sweet-tasting and beautiful, so look for them. To make your summer drinks extra fancy, freeze them in ice cubes. Red clover flowers can be dried and used to make a blood-cleansing tea that can be consumed all year. Calendula flowers can be used to make a poultice to treat cuts and burns. Violets are frequently crystallized for cake decorations, and dandelion blooms can be converted into a honey-like syrup or a blemish-healing face mask.

Summer is also the greatest time to gather leaves and stems before plants bloom. This is the greatest time to select the leaves of culinary herbs including sage, thyme, oregano, and rosemary. These plants can be useful for drying and storing for the winter. Many additional herbs, notably those known as "Italian herbs," have antibacterial characteristics that make them effective as gargles or teas if you have a respiratory illness.

Growing Herbs

Because most herbs are native to the Mediterranean, the key to promoting their growth is to create similar conditions. This implies plenty of sunlight, mild temperatures, and well-drained soil.

You may begin growing and maintaining your kitchen herb garden indoors at any time of year. If you want to develop a tiny herb corner in your garden or outdoor planter, the best time to start growing herbs is in the spring, after the threat of frost has passed.

Best Conditions

Most culinary herbs grow in full sun, with 7-8 hours of exposure – remember those Mediterranean conditions? This is the optimal time for them to create the essential oils that give them their distinctive fragrance and flavor. Some herbs, such as basil, parsley, and cilantro, may benefit from partial shade from the fiercest noon sun during the blazing summer months.

Indoors, the greatest place to cultivate herbs is beside a sunny window. If your home does not receive enough natural light, consider purchasing a grow light.

These useful additions not only offer your plant the light it requires but also encourage it to grow fuller. If you're growing fragrant herbs in containers or pots, avoid using garden soil because it doesn't give adequate drainage. Choose a well-draining organic potting mix designed exclusively for this style of growing.

Terracotta pots with drainage holes are also preferable to plastic planters because they allow for more aeration of the plants and help avoid moldy roots.

Herb plants are ideal for container gardening, and you can even grow multiple types in the same pot, with the exception of a few species (more on that later). Growing your herbs in pots has the advantage of allowing you to relocate them, ensuring that they always have perfect growing circumstances.

Before spreading your seeds, thoroughly read the seed packs. They provide a wealth of useful information, such as how much space to provide between seeds, the growing season, and the type of solar exposure they prefer.

When watering your herbs, remember that overwatering is more likely to destroy them than underwatering. Sticking your finger an inch or two into the pot is a fantastic tip for determining the soil's moisture level.

If it's still wet, don't water it. It's time to moisten your herbs if the soil is loose. Aromatic plants prefer less frequent but thorough waterings than more frequent but superficial waterings. The latter can stimulate roots to reach for water near the soil's surface, which you want to avoid. You want a deep root system that will provide stability and strength to your plant.

Seeds or Seedlings?

Like any other plant, herbs can be grown from seed or purchased as young plants — or seedlings — from your local plant nursery. Even while starting with seeds offers advantages, you may feel more confident starting with seedlings if this is your first time growing herbs. Back to the Root's kitchen herb garden kit, which comes with everything you need to create your own herb corner, is a foolproof growing kit for novices. It contains organic basil, mint, and cilantro seeds, as well as a special soil combination that delivers all of the nutrients your herbs require to grow strong and sturdy.

Back to the Roots growth kits are also backed by a no-risk gardening policy. In other words, you'll keep getting more seeds until you successfully grow your herbs.

Annual, Biennial, and Perennial Herbs

Herbs, like other plants, fall into one of three categories: annual, biennial, or perennial. It's critical to understand which plant is which to know how to treat them and what to expect when you start growing your culinary herbs.

Annual herbs: This cultivar germinates, blooms, sets seeds and dies all in the same year. They will only reappear the following year if they have dropped seeds that successfully germinate in the spring. Annual herbs include basil, cilantro, and marjoram.

Biennial herbs: These plants have a two-year life cycle, which means they germinate and grow one year, then bloom and die the following year. Biennial plants include parsley and chives.

Perennial herbs: Perennial plants live for a long time. They may continue to provide into the winter months, depending on your local climate. During the winter season, they frequently drop their leaves (which resemble dead, dry sticks) as a form of defense. Perennials return year after year, growing from roots that have survived the winter. Thyme, mint, oregano, tarragon, and lemon balm are good examples of this type.

Harvesting

Harvesting is without a doubt one of the most pleasurable and enjoyable aspects of herb farming. It's also important to promote fresh leaf and branch growth.

The best method is to cut them right above a natural junction or lead node when collecting herbs. When you do this, you stimulate new growth, which causes your plants to branch out on all sides and get fuller.

Annual herbs prefer modest, regular cuts until the end of the growing season or the first frost. On the other hand, Perennials can benefit from good pruning, especially after the warm season has begun. If you reside in a region that frequently freezes over the winter, it's better to avoid vigorous trimming after August.

When a fragrant herb begins to blossom and flower, it is usually a strong indication that it is time to start generating seeds and finally hibernate for the season.

When this happens, the edible leaves shrink, become harder, and more bitter. To postpone this, simply pinch or snip off the blossoming tips as soon as they appear. If they persist, remove the entire flowering stalk. By eliminating the blooms, you ensure that your plant's energy is directed toward producing leaves.

Simple Herbs to Get Your Herb Garden Started
Now that you've learned the fundamentals of herb cultivation, you're ready to discover which fragrant plants are the easiest and most versatile to cultivate in your environment. These are all classic herbs that will give your favorite foods a flavor boost and elevate your cooking to the next level.

1. Basil
You must plant basil if you enjoy pizza, pesto, and bruschetta. Nothing beats fresh-picked basil tossed on top of a hot Margherita pizza.

This classic Italian herb benefits from regular pruning since it encourages the plant to grow less leggy — with weak stems that make it floppy — and more rounded.

If you enjoy fresh pesto, grow a few basil plants to ensure a steady supply whenever you crave this delectable green sauce. Plant the seeds 12-16 inches apart to give the plants plenty of room to grow.

2. Chives

Chives and spring onions are the perfect savory garnish. Chopped chives go well with soups, roasted potatoes, avocado toast, and smoked salmon and cream cheese bagels.

It's one of the simplest culinary herbs to grow, and it's excellent for boosting a rookie gardener's self-esteem. When harvesting, sow them 4-6 inches apart and cut them two inches above the soil. They typically regrow in the early spring.

3. Cilantro

If you're confused between cilantro and coriander, don't worry: they're the same thing.

The leaves are referred to as cilantro, while the seeds are referred to as coriander. The mystery is solved!

This extremely adaptable herb is used in various cuisines, from Mexican to the Mediterranean to Asian. It's ideal for cutting and adding to recipes to lend a fresh, herbal flavor.

When it comes to cilantro, though, you either love it or despise it. This is due to the herb's high concentration of aldehydes, a molecule found in soap. Some people have a mutation that permits them to sense this chemical, and when they chew cilantro, they swear it tastes like a soap bar.

Plant your cilantro plants 6-8 inches apart and protect them from the intense summer sun, as they will bolt and try to shed seeds quickly.

4. Lemon Balm

Lemon balm, like chamomile, is a great relaxing herb and a great addition to your herb garden. It's a member of the mint family, and when you smell it, you'll notice a lovely combination of mint and lemon. It can be used fresh in desserts, salads, tea, and as a garnish for drinks.

It should be eaten raw, not cooked. Otherwise, it will lose its lovely aroma. It's useful in herb planting since it repels mosquitoes and other pests. It spreads like mint, so plant it alone or with another type from the same family. Allow 12-18 inches between seeds for optimum growth.

5. Mint

When you think of summer plants, the first thing that comes to mind is probably mint. This classic aromatic herb has a fresh scent that complements summer salads, drinks, and iced tea.

A traditional folk cure for an upset stomach is chew a few mint leaves or brew them in tea. This lovely herb comes in a plethora of variations, making it difficult to pick just one.

Stick to peppermint or spearmint for a more familiar scent. However, if you enjoy experimenting with other aromatic herbs, keep a lookout for chocolate mint. Its distinct smell will remind you of your favorite chocolate chip mint ice cream, and it's ideal for making warm, comforting tea in the winter.

Plant your mint within containers, as you would lemon balm, leaving 18-24 inches between the seeds.

Preparation

It's important to consider how herbs are prepared and the best method for taking them. Herbal preparations include:

- Capsules
- Poultices
- Balms and salves
- Infusions
- Tinctures
- Teas and tisanes
- Powders

The method utilized is determined by what the herb will be used for, how it will be stored, and how long you want it to last.

Herbs must be processed in order to retain their effectiveness and make their use more practical.
"

It is critical to understand that herbs have been prepared for millennia and continue to be processed before usage. "Some herbs can be

consumed fresh, but for practicality, tradition, and occasionally safety, herbs are usually prepared in some form before usage."
It should be noted that medicated ghee and oil preserve potency while preventing herbs from going to waste.
"Infusing the herb in this way can extend its shelf life by a year," she explains. "Fresh herbs may only be potent for a day or two." Tinctures are one of the greatest methods to consume herbs since they conserve potency, have a long shelf life, and, in some situations, can improve the herb's efficacy.

Tools Needed to Make Herbal Medicines

Some of these tools are commonplace objects seen in a wellstocked kitchen. Others you might have never seen or used before.

In any case, if you want to prepare more herbal teas, tinctures, salves, and other products at home, here are a few important pieces of equipment that every herbalist should have in their kitchen.

1. Scissors & Baskets

First and foremost, you will require a basket to transport your herbs and scissors to harvest them with. I adore finding baskets at thrift stores and go looking for them every time I go. Any handle-equipped basket will suffice. Herb harvesting also necessitates the use of highquality scissors, as some stems are rather thick. This pair is extremely durable and comfy, and the blades may be sharpened as needed.

2. Fine Mesh Sieve, in all different sizes

My fine mesh sieves are one of my most frequently utilized herbal instruments. I have three different sizes in a set like this, and I use them all the time! I'm always straining things in the kitchen, and I use these sieves for everything. With my potato ricer, the larger one is ideal for filtering tinctures or infused oils.

3. Potato Ricer

A potato ricer is, without a doubt, the best natural tool you can own. That's right; you read that accurately. Have you ever come across a tincture press? They are pretty pricey! The same procedure can be done using a potato ricer! When straining each tincture or infused oil, use this. It will extract every last bit of liquid from your herbs. I've had and used this potato ricer for almost 4 years and I adore it!

4. Mortar and Pestle

A mortar and pestle are both gorgeous and functional! They work incredibly well for coarsely grinding your herbs, and did I mention they're beautiful? It's a lot of fun to utilize them! You can also use a spice grinder, but I like my mortar and pestle combination.

5. Spice Grinder

I prefer to leave my herbs whole for as long as possible before grinding them when I'm ready to utilize them. This keeps them fresher for longer and keeps many of their medicinal characteristics intact. Herbal powders oxidize quickly and lose their efficacy. Keep a spice grinder on available and process your herbs as needed for the finest flavor and medicine.

You can use an electric type, or a portable grinder will suffice. I also like to stock small manual pepper grinders with herb and spice blends to grind straight into meals.

6. Kitchen Scale

Some herbal preparations, such as tinctures and teas, need you to weigh your components. You may require exact measures to ensure that you can make the tea exactly the same way the following time or ensure that you have the correct potency for your tincture. I prefer having a little kitchen scale like this one on hand. It completes the task!

7. Stainless Steel Funnel

Do you have a canning funnel? A stainless steel canning funnel is required if you wish to keep herbal recipes in mason jars.

8. Tea Press

A tea press is the most convenient way to prepare big amounts of tea. I like to make a nutritious herbal infusion with mine. I soak the infusion for several hours before pouring it off and drinking it cold or warm. The press does an excellent job of straining out all of the plant stuff! It's perfect for making huge batches of tea or my daily infusion blend. This tea press is adorable, but a coffee press will suffice! Keep your coffee apart from your tea press. Otherwise, your tea will taste like coffee as well. I have a special tea press for herbs that I exclusively use.

9. Tea Strainer

For a single cup of tea, a tea strainer is a great tool to have on hand. These stainless steel filters with lids are fantastic. They preserve your tea's aromatic volatile oils until you're ready to drink it!

10. Electric Teapot

Some may believe that this item is unnecessary. It does, however, make preparing tea a breeze rather than a burden! I always fill my electric teapot to the brim and brew several jars of tea at once. Then I either save some for later or drink many cups of tea right away. It warms water faster than you can say. "Peter Piper picked a peck of pickled peppers" ten times correctly! Okay, maybe not for some of you, but it warms water quickly!

It's nice to have a teapot that makes making tea' so much easier, especially because water is the best extractant for herbal medicines and medicine!

CHAPTER 3: USING FRESH PLANTS

Harvesting

Herb Harvesting for Drying

As long as the plant has enough leaves to maintain growth, herbs can be taken as needed throughout the growing season. Snipping the plants on a regular basis encourages new growth and keeps the herbs healthy. Limit these harvests to less than one-third of the plant in order for it to continue growing and producing new foliage. The fragrant oils in most herbs are best picked early in the morning after the dew has dissipated but before the sun's rays have evaporated.

When to Pick Herbs for Maximum Flavor and Aroma:

Herbs that will be dried for preservation should be gathered at their peak to preserve the natural oils that give the herbs their flavor, scent, and therapeutic characteristics.

The timing is determined by the plant part being harvested and how it will be used:

Foliage: Herbs planted specifically for their leaves should be collected before the plant blooms. After the plant flowers and begins to go to seed, the flavor of the leaves becomes bitter.

Flowers: When gathered shortly after flower buds develop, herbs grown for flowers have the highest oil concentration and flavor before the blooms fully open.

Seeds: Herbs planted for seeds should be gathered once the seeds have matured and dried on the plant. When they are ready, they usually turn a dark brown or black color.

How to Gather Herbs:

For drying, select healthy foliage, flowers, or seeds. Cut the stems carefully with scissors. Remove any moldy, sick, or insect-infested pieces.

Leafy Annual Herbs: Pinch off leaves from the tips of the stems just above a pair of leaves to harvest leafy annual herbs like basil and marjoram. The plant will continue to develop and sprout two branches above the leaves. This is known as "pinching off" because it stimulates the plant to grow bushier and produce more sensitive foliage. To keep the plant productive, harvest leafy tips on a regular basis and clip off flower buds. Before the first frost, harvest the entire plant.

Leafy Perennial Herbs: Thyme, sage, and tarragon are perennial herbs that can be collected by the stem or sprig. Cut the stems 3-4 inches from the plant's base to harvest the herb. Herbs with long stems, such as parsley and oregano, can be harvested by cutting the stem near the plant's base. Cut stems above a pair of leaves to harvest rosemary, which will branch out and continue to grow. Harvest perennial herbs until about four weeks before the first frost. Allow the plant to focus on winding down for the season before falling dormant as winter approaches.

Blossoms: Some herbs have single flowers, while others have clusters of blooms along a stem or spikes. Single blossoms like chamomile, calendula, and feverfew are gathered by picking the individual flowers when the flower has fully opened. When some of the blooms are open, cut the stem several inches from the base of the plant or above the top set of leaves to harvest the spiky blossoms.

Seeds: Anise, caraway, coriander, and dill are among the herbs collected for their seeds and are typically dried on the plant. Allow the herb to blossom and set seed. As the seeds dry after flowering, they expand and ripen from green to brown to black. When the seeds are dry, they are ready to harvest. When the seed head is touched, the seeds usually flow out. Place a container beneath the seed head and clip the stem so that the seed cluster and any seeds released to fall into the container.

Drying
How to Dry Herbs for Long-Term Storage

Herbs should be dried as soon as possible after harvesting to preserve essential oils and maximize flavour intensity and therapeutic advantages. Unless I see visible dust or pests, I don't rinse my herbs to add moisture. Before preserving herbs in jars, they must be well dried. A dark, warm, dust-free environment with sufficient air circulation is optimal for drying. The leaves are suitable for storage when they are dry and crumbly.

Here are a few methods for drying herbs for storage:

Hang and Air Dry Herbs: The simplest way to dry herbs with stems is to air-dry them. Tie the stems together into little bundles and hang them upside down in a dry, warm, dust-free, and airy location away from direct sunlight. I prefer to wrap elastics around the stems because they keep the bunch together even when the stems shrink after drying.

Air Dry Herbs Using a Drying Screen: Alternatively, put the herbs out to dry on a window or drying screen. Suspend the drying screen between two chairs, allowing air to circulate above and below the screen.

Use a Food Dehydrator: Our summers in Maine are humid, and the moisture in the air can hinder some herbs from naturally air-drying. To dry herbs faster, I use a food dehydrator. A dehydrator operates by gently moving air via screens. Use low heat to avoid degrading the quality of the herbs.

Further Drying Seeds: Remove the seeds from the seed heads and spread them out in a shallow layer in an open container for another 1-2 weeks to dry. Using your fingers, separate the seeds from the seed head and chaff.

I like to store the seed heads in a paper bag with a few holes punched in the top for air circulation. After a few weeks, I shake the bag vigorously to loosen the seeds from the seed head. The seeds are then separated from the dried plant material and spread out in a shallow container to dry further before storing.

How to Store Dry Herbs:

Remove the leaves from the stems and store them loosely in clean glass jars or containers with airtight lids after the herbs are dried and brittle. To preserve the flavor and strength of the herbs, do not crush or crumble them until shortly before using them. Label your jars with the herb's name and the date.

Keep your jars in a cool, dark place away from heat, humidity, and temperature changes. The kitchen cabinet, believe it or not, is not the best location to keep dry herbs. The majority of my herbs are kept in huge jars in a cool, dark, seldom-used cupboard. For the kitchen cupboard, I fill small herb jars with roughly a month's worth of herbs. When stored properly, dried herbs will keep their potency for at least six to twelve months.

CHAPTER 4: EXTRACTIONS

Several procedures must be carried out to achieve a suitable concentration of the active ingredients in the plants and for their action to be more effective. The active ingredients must be extracted using appropriate solvents chosen based on the solubility and stability of the beneficial substances.

Extraction processes allow for the creation of pharmaceutical ingredients suitable for oral or external administration based on the desired site of action.

Decoctions, infusions, fluid extracts, dense or dry (depending on liquid content), and tinctures are the various types of herbal preparations. They are also known as galenic formulations, after the forefather of plant-based medicinal creation, Claudius Galen.

Extractive techniques that allow obtaining active ingredients in pure form for more sophisticated medication processing: pills, liquids, ointments, capsules, and so on, have been developed from these procedures, but they have failed to displace the original preparations, which are currently more popular because they are more innocuous and have fewer unwanted reactions.

To ensure the quality of these preparations, which do not require as exact control as licensed pharmaceuticals, pharmacopeias have included scientifically based regulations within their specifications; however, some care must be taken in terms of preservation and storage time.
Because of the ease of preparation and the medicinal plant's availability at any time, immediate usage is encouraged.
The plant must be carefully cleaned before extraction treatment to avoid contamination from other plants or other mechanical particles. The purpose is to extract compounds using menstruum solvent, which is a suitable solvent. Medicinal plants are becoming more important as a source of therapeutic compounds, which could lead to the development of novel drugs.

The bulk of these components, such as phenolics and flavonoids, have been found to offer health benefits, including cancer prevention. The presence of phenolic and flavonoid compounds in medicinal plants has been linked to antioxidant activity, which is important in the prevention of age-related disorders, particularly those caused by oxidative stress.

The pharmaceutical and cosmetic industries rely on phytochemicals present in medicinal plants. Extraction is the process of isolating medicinally useful mixtures of a variety of plant metabolites, such as alkaloids, glycosides, phenolics, terpenoids, and flavonoids, using selected solvents and well-established procedures. All solvent extraction methods try to isolate soluble plant compounds while leaving the insoluble cellular marc behind. The following are the most common extraction procedures.

Maceration, infusion, percolation, and decoction

The maceration extraction method is utilized in the production of wine and the extraction of bioactive components from plants. Maceration entailed soaking plant materials (coarse or powdered) in a stoppered container with a solvent for at least 3 days with regular agitation, followed by pressing or straining and filtration.

Heat is delivered via convection and conduction in traditional procedures, and the solvent is chosen based on the substance to be extracted. Infusion and decoction work on maceration's same principles; however, they are both steeped in cold or boiled water.

A decoction is only ideal for extracting heat-stable chemicals and hard plant components such as roots and barks. The procedure often yielded more oil-soluble compounds than maceration and infusion.

Aromatherapy and Flower Essences

Essential oils and flower essences are two fantastic ways to reap the therapeutic benefits of nature. Have you ever noticed how a scent may carry you back in time to where you first encountered it? Or how the aroma of apple pie brings you to your grandmother's house? Aromas can have far-reaching effects on the body and mind. Aromatherapy, which makes use of essential oils, can have a significant impact on your physical and emotional health.

Flower essences have a high potency as well. They are extremely effective for healing from a wide range of emotional and mental illnesses, from the most basic to the most complicated. Because our emotions can have a physical impact on us, they can also aid in the healing of physical disorders. Let's have a look at these two healing approaches!

Essential Oils

For therapeutic purposes, essential oils are produced from aromatic plants. The oils can be found in various plant parts, including leaves, seeds, flowers, roots, and bark. One of the most prevalent ways of obtaining oils from plants is steam distillation. If done correctly, the oils will keep their entire strength and character.

Essential oils are not to be confused with perfume. They are therapeutic-grade oils. Although essential oils were used to make perfume in ancient societies, current fragrances are mostly chemical impersonations.

In fact, any skin or cosmetic product that uses the term "fragrance" without mentioning where the fragrance derives from is either a chemical imitation or contains chemical boosters to "extend" the scent. These boosters frequently contain hazardous substances such as phthalates, which are recognized hormone disruptors.

The quality, purity, and authenticity of essential oils should be of the utmost significance to anyone who intends to use them to accomplish a specific result. The plants themselves are the source of the quality. In their native environment, the plants must be strong, healthy, and prospering. They must be harvested at the appropriate time of year and at the appropriate time of day. For each variety of plants, the best extraction method must be identified. The oils must be securely stored—in glass bottles, away from heat and light.

These essential oils will be more expensive but significantly superior in quality.

If utilized inappropriately, certain natural chemical elements of essential oils, such as phenols and ketones, might be harmful. Phenols are strong antiseptics and bactericides. Therefore oils containing them should be used sparingly and for short periods of time. Basil, clove, oregano, and thyme are phenol-rich oils. Ketones are cell-regenerative and aid in the breakdown of mucus and lipids. Because of potential safety concerns, they should be used in moderation and avoided during pregnancy. Ketone-containing oils include sage, cedar leaf, peppermint, and fennel. Quality oils can be very potent, so keep them out of the reach of youngsters, take caution around pets, and keep them away from the eyes.

Pure, undiluted oils can be stored for years if kept in a cold, dry place and well closed. Oils that are improperly stored can oxidize and become rancid.

Essential oils can be used in a variety of applications. You can disseminate the aroma using a diffuser with a cool air stream or by gently warming the oil. Oils can also be inhaled directly from the bottle. If the oil isn't too potent, you can place a few drops on a cotton ball, seal it in a baggie, and sniff it. This method keeps the oils potent for about a week.

Some oils can be used directly to the skin, but consult with a skilled source first. Oils are typically diluted in a carrier oil such as grapeseed, jojoba, almond, apricot kernel, coconut, or another oil. It is critical to use a high-quality, skin-nourishing oil. After that, the mixture can be used for massage, a chest rub, a foot rub, or as a body oil. Oils can also be used in the bath, sauna, or as a foot soak. Many of the oils are also suitable for use as perfume.

The nicest part about the oils is that they have therapeutic benefits in addition to their lovely, soothing fragrances.

Some common conditions and the oils that are indicated for them are listed below.

Here are a few examples:
Antivirals— Lemon, Lavenders, Bay Laurel, Cinnamon Bark, Clove Bud, Eucalyptus, Tea Tree, Ravensara, Thyme.
Antibacterials—Clove Bud, or Cinnamon Bark, Oregano, Thyme, Eucalyptus.
Stress Relief—Sandalwood, Rose, Clary Sage, Frankincense, Bergamot, Chamomile, Lavender, Black Spruce, Vanilla, or Vetiver, Fir, Ylang Ylang, Cedar, Geranium, Jasmine, Orange Sweet,
Patchouli, Basil. Oshadhi's Anxiety Rescue, Balancing, Meditation, Peace & Quiet, Peace of Mind, and Stress Relief blends are excellent for stress relief.
Fatigue—Black Spruce, Ginger, Tea Tree, Lemon, Rosemary, Black Pepper, Eucalyptus, Peppermint, Pine, or Thyme.

Motivation—Tea Tree, or Thyme, Rosemary, Clove, Morning Motivation and Prosperity will also get you started.

Concentration/Mental Clarity—Basil, Peppermint, Rosemary, Lemon, Eucalyptus Globulus, or Thyme. Clarity is an excellent combination oil for studying and focusing.

Flower Essences

A flower essence is exactly what it sounds like: a flower's essence. They are potentized liquid plant medicines that bear the direct imprint of a flower. Flower essences, unlike vitamins, focus on the emotional or energetic body rather than the physical body. There is a floral essence for almost every emotional or mental ailment known to man. They were invented in the 1930s by Dr. Edward Bach. Some people are familiar with the Bach flower essences, but there are many more flower essence lines as well.

Flower essences are created by collecting flowers at their pinnacle of bloom and infusing them with water when they are laid in water in the sunlight. The energy of the flower is therefore transferred to the water. A mother tincture is created, which is subsequently diluted to stock level. After that, it is preserved using alcohol.

Flower essences are extraordinarily mild. They have a mild effect on the emotional body. They do not interact with any vitamin, herb, homeopathic cure, or prescription medicine. They are also suitable for children due to their soft nature.

People, particularly children, are excellent at selecting their own floral essences. Children, in general, are more in tune with their intuition and excel at it. You can choose an essence by researching a specific topic and discovering which essences are associated with it. There could be more than one essence that speaks to you. You can mix up to seven essences at once. There are also pre-made combos that can help with concerns such as grieving, motivation, and heart opening.

Flower essences can be placed under your tongue or mixed into water and sipped throughout the day. It is critical to take the essences at least twice a day and to be cognizant of why you are taking them.

When using a floral essence, make sure you finish the bottle unless you have a sensation that you are finished with the problem. Improvement on an issue is often minor, but once a bottle is finished, you should notice a difference.

As I previously stated, literally hundreds of essences can help with practically any mental or emotional difficulty you may be experiencing.

Here are a few examples:

Buttercup— Reduces feelings of low self-worth, the inability to see your individuality, and the need for external recognition or renown. Elm— Assists those who feel unequal to the burden of personal or professional commitments. It alleviates feelings of overwhelm and gives you the trust and confidence to persevere.

Gorse— Increases optimism by enhancing the positive traits of conviction and hope. Especially beneficial for those concerned about the state of the world and have difficulty envisioning positive possibilities.
Impatiens– Reduces impatience, anger, intolerance, and the constant feeling that there isn't enough time. Allows us to be in tune with our daily rhythms, life events, and the speed of others.
Pretty Face— For people who believe they have been rejected because of their physical appearance. Increases the emphasis on inner beauty.

CONCLUSION

With over 2,000 indigenous tribes in North America, healing traditions varied considerably from tribe to tribe, involving a diverse spectrum of ceremonies, rites, and healing expertise. While there were no final healing requirements, most tribes believed that health was a spiritual expression and a never-ending process of keeping spiritually, emotionally, and physically healthy. This power and harmony with oneself, others, nature, and one's Creator would keep illness and damage at bay. Everyone was responsible for their own health, and all actions and thoughts had consequences, such as illness, disability, bad luck, or trauma. Their health could only be healed by restoring harmony.

Herbal therapies played a significant role in these therapeutic practices, going beyond physical aches and pains and into realms of spirituality and harmony.

Herbs and other natural materials used in medicines were often collected from their surroundings, resulting in a variety of remedies. Commodities that were unavailable locally, on the other hand, were occasionally exchanged over long distances. Herbs and therapeutic plants were commonly held in high respect.

Many of the many techniques have been passed down orally from generation to generation and have never been written down. As a result, many pharmaceutical remedies remain a mystery. In rare circumstances, healers who established a written language, such as the Cherokee, wrote down their formulas or methods.

When early Europeans arrived in the United States more than 500 years ago, they were surprised to find Native Americans recuperating from illnesses and injuries they had assumed were deadly. In many aspects, the Indians' herbal treatments were far superior to those known to the newcomers. The Native Americans, on the other hand, had no remedies for the "afflictions of civilization," or white man's diseases such as measles and smallpox, which would kill millions of them over the next few decades.

Not only were these many Native Americans lost, but so were bodies of knowledge that went to the grave with healers. Despite the loss of some information, much of it has survived and is used by both Native Americans and non-natives today.

Many modern medicines are developed from plants and herbs that have been used for thousands of years by Indians. Indeed, approximately 200 Native American botanicals have been or are now employed in pharmaceuticals.

Today's medical philosophy is shifting toward an approach that recognizes and respects every unique component, including mental and spiritual dimensions. As a result, both natives and non-natives are regaining interest in Native American medical practices.

Many people are turning to natural herbal remedies because they are concerned about the toxicity, addictive qualities, and negative side effects of pharmaceutical treatments. For millennia, quality Native American items have been developed and used to treat a range of ailments. While this is not always the case, herbal therapies are often less toxic and have fewer unpleasant side effects than many prescription medications. When looking for herbal remedies, look for well-managed and created products that use only the highest quality organic ingredients and follow stringent pharmaceutical manufacturing requirements.